Chora.

Sandra Doller

AHSAHTA PRESS

BOISE STATE UNIVERSITY • BOISE • IDAHO • 2010

Ahsahta Press, Boise State University
Boise, Idaho 83725
http://ahsahtapress.boisestate.edu
http://ahsahtapress.boisestate.edu/books/sdoller/sdoller.htm

Printed in the United States of America
Cover design by Quemadura
Front cover art: from Yanira Castro's dance and audio installation "(fetus)twin," presented at the Choc-
    olate Factory in Long Island City. Performer: Nancy Ellis. Photograph: Charles Merritt Houghton.
Back cover photograph: Ben Doller
Book design by Janet Holmes
First printing January 2010
ISBN-13: 978-1-934103-12-8

Library of Congress Cataloging-in-Publication Data

Doller, Sandra, 1974-
Chora / Sandra Doller.
    p. cm. — (The new series ; no. 33)
ISBN-13: 978-1-934103-12-8 (pbk. : alk. paper)
ISBN-10: 1-934103-12-8 (pbk. : alk. paper)
I. Title.
PS3613.I5529C48 2010
811'.6—DC22

                            2009042085

ACKNOWLEDGMENTS

Grateful thanks to the editors of the following fine magazines, in which some of these poems first
appeared: *Aufgabe, The Canary, Crowd, Cut Bank, Denver Quarterly, Equilibrium, Forklift Ohio, La
Petite Zine, New Orleans Review, Octopus, Order & Decorum, Parcel, The Poetry Project Newsletter,
Verse,* and *Xantippe.* Support small presses & mags—they support you!

This book was generously supported by a Paul Engle–James Michener Fellowship from the University
of Iowa Writers' Workshop and a University Professional Development grant from California State
University–San Marcos.

Big thanks are also due to my heroines, without whom I would have neither the notion nor the
space: Rae Armantrout, Mei-Mei Berssenbrugge, Lee Ann Brown, Yanira Castro, Constance Congdon,
Janet Holmes, Fanny Howe, Susan Maxwell, Tracie Morris, Claudia Rankine, Leslie Scalapino, Cole
Swensen, Wendy Woodson.

Odetta: 1930-2008.

Chora.

Ahsahta Press

The New Series

Number 33

for Ben,
again.

Table of Contents.

Chora.

Like i'm about to get on
a really long train

the train that i'm talking about
go open
through oakland

a train over the ocean
i don't mean a lake
a train over the sea

tee-pee on the beach
tires in the water
shanties
rock tunnel
mountains yillow

a barge out there
they're out there
orange warship
lead to warship

can i get a witness
can i get a weakness

everything that was dark is
light
like bridge

green rocks
sticks out of water
keep out shacks
rusted equi-prints
sun

register the noises
sun on top of water
next to lines of geese
next to gulls

sun mixed with water
brick water
sediment fish
& herons

gills
laid track
sit up

i saw the most beautiful
tires

i had to call
the sea at martinez
excess

we sell
hot breakfast
fresh food
1258
we stoop and stand

in the high excess
the column wrote
rosy

stand back
shore

if you have visitors
please exit with him

the conductress
no visitors

not on the ocean
sea of men

cars stand hardly broken
where you were not

sea dot
a tint bitter
you would have seen it

millions of omens
one mouth

orange hillsides
slides the bay

hello sugar
train through ocean runs
pass through throat

the ocean's crew
limit the union
3 brief moments

soft steamboat
often rolling
welcome to martinez

that hill over there
i am in the wrong car
trucks over truckee

can i get witnessed
i was riding over
no one is driving
i have a specialty

the thing to do
in the yellow hills
hang like wasps.

Unexpected particle
blessed one-sided Morning

A here
let me
in front of it stand
Beselved

A sylvan nearing
the throaty Clime

That water strip
in scrubby green
no horn calls it
lacy Music

The lousy south
window in a tree
go in
parade the View

Racy tonal dye
makes a foxy end
sunset is private Cup

Pupil of the fuzz
that fruit they call two fruits
escapable
for Dinner

They had dinner
a number of confusions
Ensue

I had been out-lonesomed
so far
a migrant
baker
in the room
his last name
we Recorded

The migrant baker
on the porch
where he double-lives
in ecstasy of fur
red or white
or Blonde

No serious hill rises
no serial anatomies
bring your color over
fetch Us

An awful high
to Bear

Told to wolf
tell it
with glad eyes
orphan annie Eyes

What *kind* of Pointing?
What *kind* of Horns?

he works for a smithy
where did you get that hammer
i need a lot of help

he's the one who customizes
your swords

can you help me a bit
on my game

i'm a little bit
only
the mist that sits there

i have no idea
i didn't see the fence

the bad bad guy
you do not mind his argument

a squirrel that follows
many guitars

this was short
timely
columnar

do not sight the Alps
do not leave your house
had i a way

i'm just happy we killed a ghost
and then what

why do you have to have to
& what is the adjective of lamb?

children
no more
for the sun

i had a curfew
a curriculum
and curves

we go west
we go

tonight they will loudly
mull it

green is the color
yellow is the color
blue is the color
what rose

'I am about everything.'
'Don't you envy me?'

nothing out there in the grass
didn't tumble her

1st Friends Quaker Meeting, chapter, something about the mental life being the only life, how the world tells us to do do, the great silence, most people with eyes, I alternated & it's pretty much like a bunch of people in a movie theater, but there's no movie, the mind. Then someone spoke about about a novel in which someone said: people suffer because they want things to be different than they are, as there are no answers & maybe even no responses, different from the silence of a shark. Then much later a woman, then the guy with the question got up & left. Woman speaks about her grandson being teased for being soft & delicate, her Quaker uncle being tortured for refusing going to war in WWI, she said she prays for men to be allowed & for women to encourage, she talked about Thomas, what you bring forth will save you, what you do not bring forth... I thought about the inevitability. Then a guy spoke about hearing things, across the room, like those rooms where you position yourself perfectly to hear from a distance, about mishearing being the only kind of hearing. What about form & structure, then the silent part was over & people started shaking hands but the people in front of me turned around & looked at me but didn't shake my hand, but then another woman came over & shook my hand, then they got announcements & I left.

seeking havoc
the man wants to kill me
still
waiting at the grange

wouldn't hurt to
stood
bruising
thick salt hands

of the ear
her recollections of *f* are off
madam
i was substitute
d
with a cigar

my car drives me
south
so south

at the party a party
a holder

borderline hair
& martyrs
tell me more

prairie pounder
in thunder
hold
in number

please review
your luggage

what carry
what carry you

keep tiding
i am huge

nails
the croissant
to the cross

nails nothing

go ahead neighbor
pucker

cloudlings
catcher
the bottom of the pit
of the air

i hadn't pitched
anything
yet

until the 3 songs
bear
easy easy

always
to the edges
8 hops

you are enormous
all over me

pineapple
some stickers
i had sleeves

or not
on a cloud
at the museum
of listen

take me
it said
feed me blisters &
seedlings

ceilings over
the air
anatural living
harder than sky plaster

plenty of ceiling
for all
of you

a missed midwest
slightly easter
than thou

math is true
you know honest ice

your face parks
love your eyecones
how myopia

the white on white package
serious boots
a moustachio

six times nine
you are free to move

swatches blue
through white seen
seems above

like the arctic nothing
skirt
over a bodice
often you
the body
stamped land
glower

radio tower white
simple mind blue
deck of cards black
house green

what is that plastic spot
a single nipple on earth
from here

the phone in me says
go
with tambour hair

here is a case
for you

may you simple
viral
perfection
under microscope cope

could you get to me

red gross hills
children rack

      everything
      is from a can
      one tin

Midi

the logic of mending/road's long

double double

the tim timothy bunches

+ cymbals where where they shouldn't be

the valley's tergum

clings

finite + visible/she'll operatic and

odd margins this box is visibles and

as margins vines become/the major

the panga

oh the substance

negative musk musk people don't

burnish with cloth/scraps

beautiful hump

midday/riot in the gym the same

leather happen

Ruth Brown valley

neither is the shady vox in the open savanna

open to ask a snare or ask

to snare itself

that librettiste one parts ruby

to twelve parts/rouge is red there.

Middle bind
      of the symmetry road/tight like that talks
            a country highway
                  a slender and sinuous hart

core body of the girl with a yellow dress on and a kind of sign to be read if
                  time as a trumpet with a Harmon muted

fluffs split flurries
      little blistered punchers/eaten away spine edges of the flurried notes
            i subsiding into little ragged edges of breathe

as edges tell of the line become blistered/eaten away by traffic can
              center the weather
                which is later canon which is future

talking white body at 11 a.m. or high noon tinged with
              with yellow/the curtains wind
                dear late afternoon

sway toward evening/orange columnar curtains with the dress of a different
            other color on
              Ray Charles attention color

and is this body coming bound or going and does this body know you how to
read by a sign and can a sign

read by itself
where's been the melody that's been
turned split inside out and played/playing once over and over.

Tangle of the light/tight like epistle
that different color light letter/little
country hello tangle/tangential read
oranger color so/high slender and a
message to you/occupied light like i
was future as a trumpet/tangle in the
scene/edgy little letter melody/notes
to the edges of the gel/how are you/
next to the harmonica/copper eating
away the other colors/tangle papers
traffic/in scenario ragged girl with o
range dress on/Laverne Baker hiway
what is the future of slender/and can
a tangle in the note read itself/how go
your sinuous eaters there/flocks of the
pasture body of the girl with a yellow
color on inside out/dress on and kind
tangent to itself a greeting there/play
in the tune to be read/to over + over

By the tangle/why slim night on a
message like/that dress on twice th
at mess/the other colors occupied
inside the body/of the girl/of the g
el an inside narrato/how slender th
e edge copper eats at all colors/oth
erwise how are you/ragy little letter
your simple away heights this letter/
hello country hello/gal/by ruth mo
untain/knock out/an epistle by the
slender hi hiway/Go Queenie hiway
traffic in paper was past/fast tangle
would eat away at you on a night/
like copper/eats an arrow/eats at
brass/read to me a greeting dress
orange oranger/what is the future
broadcast of this scenario/the girl
's pasture was over/there a way a
hi up way/like epistle waiting read

Over & over
  symmetrical push/which ruby's
      a highway which
          moves without you/ by ruby's ending time

painted over torn sign poor little yellow line a kind of over to be muted each
                    time trumpets core

a core yellow sub
  ragged with your name/on the spine of the listener boing
            rowing on top of the road in little edges

edges little lines becoming eaten/far away someone kicked
              center by the can
                which is now in the can which is

the body is a can & talking/tinged with anything but
              white/dear mellow after but
                    later the center century

allay hanging in the window/what columns of difference a dress sports
                others color in
                    Slim Harpo a difference a

coming/but is this can center or edges and can you tell you how to hang
                by a name in a sign can a core

read a spine
       where's the listener that's sub
              split up by color offsides and playing/holding onto body else.

Demi

chorus lending/arch/road's long

say so

wall sounds blows cool

+ i cannot work where i shouldn't be

alley candle clings

miles

ninety + miss a little/the frost

miss the margins the season rakes

as war width hollers close/how corporal

the stinger

matures the oh

narrative bruise repeats people

don't buff with stone/people

slumber coral

in the gym/a tergum same time

this leather's a riot

Sam Cooke cul-de-sac

there will be in the stirring of the vocal vain

open to stone's throw's throw

to throw oneself

into the valley cool candle to

sever one's parts/there is a home there.

Quaker meeting today, too much noise, difficult to concentrate, wood grain, pink rag pillow in front of me, many people, doors opening, eyes burning when I look at them the older women, their heads raised or bowed, woman spoke about the war, the responsibility, the sadness, the what can you do of it, southern man talked about Falluja and the pictures of the children killed, he talked about Quaker prayer = what can I do, what can we do?, that is Quaker prayer, not intercessional 'inferior' prayer, where you ask 'god' to do. This I did not know. But then, then a child walked into the house, a child with problems, with glasses, with his mother, limped in, like an answer, to the meeting house, then a woman talked about Palestine, pray for them too, there is nothing else to do, is there nothing else to do? I mean, it doesn't really matter if there's a god, the apostle is chosen to speak for god, the genius serves something else, & where were the people speaking? Then the young guy talked about pacifism not being passive, a struggling for justice inherent in the pacifist position, then the woman talked about child abuse, how women have for thousands of years sat back & allowed their children to be abused, how she went to a march on D.C., how what is feminine is crushed, compassion, & this leads to atrocity, war, mass . . . also, the good morning part, & the pot luck, & where were all the people? I wonder what the old women thought of these speeches.

i had a hand
the court
an earl stole it
the lamb
the lamb
i eye you
while you play with my hand
in the corner
at your tiny
table
the earl
of no-good
the earl
of up-to-somethin
the smudge
happy
i couldn't
swallow
sparrows

dawn carries the train
weird bird
sans wing.

my adobe is no longer whiter.

we had plenty of company
we had enough.

a corporal of number
coral in nature.

the chickens killy
in the yard.

once we saw that sage
covers the planet floor
we no longer felt
greedy.

except for 3.

where will you get your cañon
next rock that swallows you.

rust
little water to go around
goes around.

some apricots
thrill to the water
pit a tunnel
to get them.

neptune honking
had about it
a brook
hooked in her
nevada
held long smoke
like traveling
together.

a hydrating force
follows him
through reno
the thickness
of a ruby
if you've seen one.

the famiglia botanica
thieved up aurora
i have a question
for the desert
i'm laying low.

love's love liest
drawl
sip no more
the unreflected sky.

'Have you altered any since I have seen you.
Isn't it a funny question for one friend to ask another.'

been a mit
before
the wastrel gets her prey
chapter seven
sere loots several
mellow margins.

'You know there is no account of her death in the Bible, and why am I not Eve?'

i'd rather be
santa claus
thanks for the news.

the passengers
the baggagers
the baggengers
the luggengers
the luggagers
will kill me
killy kill kill.

the second the engine died
the crew expired
named for eating each other.

the desert is my animal
lady

woke up to
a desert mound
with an H
& a small pyramid
on the desert

pancake clouds
2-dimensional hangers

blue hap sky
voltage
the been

some mounds red
2-dimensional
the logic of it

you cannot know
red

from future red

you cannot know
what truck
yellow machine
in the sage crop

swarms of black fly
pounds of flies
from sharpest sage

you can
know not
privileges of green
insects having at you

we will all be jackrabbit
with proof

a knowledge of such summer
a 'mind of' it
mind & motion similarly dusty

rocky girly weather
over the knee

to the edge
of the bank
of long green

remove your pesos
from my tabla

the sickening sky emblued
all over us
our palms were set stones

we _____ed with them
precious sages
verdy serpentines

more slash & slicker ensovereigned
sere a stealth rabbit slim
crosses hatches across elk and earl
the duke of desert & the ruddy route

pleased piñons empained our
perceivers go that rapine
skater lambly sleeps a pocket
in castlerock shiprock
shapelyrock grew gorgeous with eve
the mounts and mounds attendant
on diamond ease camp ducked

a town of discardies
oil drums not pennies
copper locker
house goes up comes down
a sign for not travelers

playtruck is blue in
the whole thing yard
timing thinking a red one
no bodies evidence of

hard slobber on a grand door
these mover vehicles got here
fresh oil somewhere
rocks red in the distance
smooth the brow of the tamer
town lingers long after water

east granite point smoke lies
had us a cup of it in quick sugars
sister sipping the back of blue
embarcadero plenties have few

measured matter by his bushes
gin spoke in the turner
rood age she will never leave
echo stance in large sentences

no schedule
on the train
three birds

on the other train

fierce puckered mountain
corrugated rain shack
a hard winner

wonders the stone
in his head
wonders she supplements
supplies from the tunnel

more red trucks
abandon
stacked cedar woowoo

towns containing no people
some goats
selfish oak

selvage palmetto
horse pleas

a head of two orders
the third was rushes
from that river
when there was water

out the window
an L on a hillside
an H & an L
separated by miles and track rectitude
a perfect capital on the mound
well formed if slightly stubborn
in the sun

on that hillside
cows sunsetter
rescue the plain
from its plenitude

a pan of mountain
easy contraption
in the winter when the clouds cuts
lost thirsty river
hold on
hello

the desert trucks
8 movements eastward
to get to your circle hives

thin trees of pamlico
do you not see
my exmachinery
tag factory
where is your sun

i will not do plenty more
i will wonderfull stand
with glasses

red hides its capital
into the dirt silence

i can neglect red
we never have it
without that speed

waking to finitude
to orange & oranger
i had come down to

houses in the middle off their landstar
orphans are for trains
we are here

out there
north of summer
north of sun

modify this
present

an ensemble the red of
mixtures are in

they go to bed with gilda
they go to bed with rita
they go to bed

in the beds they all go to
gilda lies
gilda lies anywhere

rita does not lie
go to bed with gilda
leave rita alone

they wake up with me
they wake up in make up
that made them

darling swifts
the lighted bird landed
at me
in each street
you pass one

the ice
it squeaks
it praises

sound of walking down stairs
sound of walking down stairs

not that
not that they're good
they're plenty

I can be applied
to anyone

an ordinary
undercover
candle
the bush
she holds a thousand
in her mouth

what house will he handle
next
what houses the sea
a dirty bloom
you have big thought
get rid of
your niches
turn up
your collar
sing for her

in the open
take away
the blue
if you could vet
a single mote
swing it

a substance
sticks
give me room
to play cards
an acre

i'll talk to you
tomorrow
when she opens
a door

i had a
too
one time
the minute
you started
to yellow
withhold
the gold
from her

her old mare nightly
breathes
a tune to the wallpaper
to turn it
a june room
enceilinged

the couple of singers
in separate corners

the belle
cassiope
withdrawing

from

Of leaping
tympan syndrome

Stricken
like all new york

Girls
i wore a tutu
tutu we're not in

That woman had no name
it was not that we did not know her name
she had none

We whisked attitudes
with
we with whisked
maturities

A child is born an ovary
he wears his ovaries on his sleeve
on his arm

A critter
pauses

A hem of some sum
keeps her from us
does the on purpose breaking of the strand
make thousands closer

Caracas
caracas' hope

Gravure
said here alters
pass over

Silent shrill
a shell fish
i was holding

In his violent dream he was the victor
the vicar
of boom

I would not be so
if i were you

I am you

Purdee helpless
perdita
at 19

At 19
i do not understand loess
what you carry in your kitty
when i was 17

Dressed in far flung floral
o caste system, speak to me
the american wastrel

Carry on
this necklace will tell you who stole it

the 5 million griffes

Tell me who you mar

It's
pellucid
grammed
tinted falling with no sound

A different sound on hitting
than you thought

Have but one
but one rock that is not for throwing

Or sounding
i am finished
we said
take it away

girls
inside girls

a field of beanfield
snakes you

end of the rime of the
furrier

we got the postcard
we got
your card

from signed

arusha
a tanzanian belt

a cape
for my face

your eyes
my face
a cape

i have never
been

hatched
as a doll

best
thigh cactus

slashes
& s's

remember
for once
once for
veronica

your veronica
hatched
here
swelled

we haven't got
much time for
faces on aprons

we all
wanted to know
your fair
your buttons

i have not
got down to
a beautiful plum
enough

a looking down
will solve it

salve the sky
with
beach blister
i mean sun
i mean it
more

hook your particles
to me

mary
quite
how did she get so
down to

i will never
tell

this was the day
this
thievy
my pet

a natural

we had wandered
so far
from macchu picchu
to say it

dear john
he never writes
like sculpture
in a garden
going under

sigh
the corpse
in the grass
you don't see

gouge
one sea
one sea fence
over
we're all goin over some day.

blanks turn into blonde
blank seats into blonde girls
the swissest.

where is the canada
region.

mention the season.

be sure
where does this take us.

i remember living
like this.

146 people are going to
ohio today.

daddy
no better window.

this mess
belongs to you.

change scars
too many people
all wink.

pull a mask
in october.

2,048
customer quo.

she is dying
to talk.

600 possible
please don't do that.

to your hair
in front of me.

you've got a presentation
so
you.

chapter crying
a baby.

single blah.

i cook east
you cook the rest.

fine dark
and hands reaching
up.

erry arms
this is me
this is me with you
this is me again.

red orphan
orphan hair
adopted 6 small legs.

we hitchhiked
wearing lavender
simplebuttondresses.

she was dressed in her
soapy
some braids.

geography
is imaginary.

flight for
this triangular.

i wan my golden arm.

wear the vice
out.

news about flying
she listens to her mother.

three of them
absent molecule
spectacle shin.

he works rodeo
wood.

don't say anything
they'll say it back.

bend with wood
take out yr
sandwich
(this time my hat was larger).

i hardly noticed
the rub.

the oldest one had glasses
(the oldest had no glasses).

made beads
decorated
her littlers
their voices are mine
they talk to themselves
bracelets.

he makes the best
national
simply ruddy
rusty.

so what's my problem
can you help me blinks
brown coal
lignite
subbituminous fallacy.

mise en abîme
sits opposite
paradox.

some thing same thing
sets opposite
its opposite.

hd's not eating of chickens
because of her love of cats

hd's not not eating of chickens
because of love of chickens

hd's not love of cats or chickens
canned

cat wing
cat thigh

hd in vienna
also saving
crema from the night before
hotel style buns

hot style buns & cigarettes
while not being a chain

the way he holds his fingers because crazy
in the hospital held his fingers like crazy

hd tea & buns & cigarettes
bryher cigar & proprietor

cigarettes were egyptian
tea was tea

expensive flowers to eat lower
material made for dresses
string bags from greece times two
leather bag sent
how swiss & spare

why not buy a new bag
$5000 costing dress
antique rings
modern hair
ubiquitous fur

never visit the old places
old little old papa
said come here

who cares about dreams & religion
why was there a baby in a box

no one thought the reeds was a casket
dead wood
size of a baby size of a cat
why care about cats

i spoke with _____ who agrees with me
mellow celebrity

can you be fortunate
& in all else wild

he was in the hospital
where his fingers were

so why does the march
in the neighbor's yard
look slightly

a crabbing
only
lawns between

she was tired
the rest of us
wanted her to stop reminding us

it takes this long to make a colored disk
being opposite
concepts

east street each
afternoon

fills with furniture
not mine

how he could not
be troubled

like three in a tree
when they passed us

do you not see
the elbows

missed golden
missed each
hospital season

hard sob of grass
seasonal disk

what color monks
were they

i had not spent
my time

We hunter the excuser
we hunter the tree

some laundry was not being done
& its implications

its it's

'tis ack
pracktackle

we winter here
verbiger
& free

aspirante
tied up in trees

& your car was wooden
you did not know better
in the dream

a full jar of heroines
am i to be blamed for
aspen spring

please dispute plenty
you stop off for
you hold on for
place the bags on the floor

he lifted up
his lief

a buoy
an extra
a tarnish

plenty
stops no man

organize the orange
landing

take care of the bees
see to the tumble
make your face shaped square

tell me about it.

Quaker meeting again today, again no one talked, there were 2 small holes in the wood on the bench in front of me, in the wood in front of me, one pointed holes, single minded & two, breathing was in two, did not go all in for the afterwards, fellowship, not pressed, how to live, not to be told how to live, how to live, how to rhythm & how to live, how to pace, if it's not a trick then what's the hurry, what's the desperate hurry, not to be tricked & the hurry. & saw, saw the sign on the wall about keeping the clutter out, these are the one-thing-a-day signs, there was the construction noise outside & clutter, & here we are inside, how to keep the outside outside & the inside in, there is crossover & penetration, but still, we still all sat in stillness, no one commented on the noise, & it was even forgettable at times, although now at home, still hearing it.

the cornices of a
cow
blond
no more darknesses

this side of the train
funicular husband
has disbanded

discards the sun
for spittle

that the grey sheets mornings
help your horizonas
is irrelevant
to the alewife
in the greener

ye starved companions
have ye left the car crash
stripped ye blankets
of their eidol.

he wears what are called
rabbits on his ears.

i got red dirt sick red clay
show me your thumbs
in glass.

m'étoile—

the rocks are not disgusting
the owl walks.

the surgery we
perform
on each other
an opera.

the phantasmatic suburb
pandemonial red-shirted crowd
or fevered condition—

marvellous
these dark rooms
a goblinstoria—

ghosts into thought
burning up the british
with a mirror.

How to Raise a Ghost
How to Use It

two glasses of blood
a bottle of vitriol
twelve drops of aqua fortis
two numbers of the journal
a small livid
some sparrow feathers
a young fop
a few grains of phosphorous
a dozen butterflies—

asked to see the shade
i had a recipe for that.

L'Ami des Lois
Galerie de la Femme Invisible

a ventriloquism
a speaking-tube
an invisible glass harmonica—

a somber incoherent speech
a metamorphosis—

there was not one quai
been crying.

.

an avulsion

a senior empty

what is the sea
but rhythm

and at the bottom of that—
grasses—

alternumerics—
mathes

i had only stood by the sycamore
for spite

i had only stood
a slim liver

the tiles on her faces
aces

cracked

a new crustiness
appears

an appeasing ease
without bard

sin bardic

solamente
fabulous
phatic ocean

the violence
is only hem

in the terrible deep
nothing crashes

vaunting
safe
sand

&

wish
you
were
sphere

so

no

matter

where

i

landed

soft
sphere

do you see me
breaking the cave
this ending

i have been sent
to inform you
of your smallness

i

remind you
of smaller things

your eyes cannot
track me down
i am violence
in your ear

milton order
of things

we should be
so unhappy.

what great open door through
the ocean spat strands of this

nestling buttercup she with her ocean-
shaped once gave us the
floor to get close & personal

with what open door greatness
loaded what harbor of liquor

gushes the jug jugs were lined
up on the fence picketly

imago moronic butterfly
with its ear to the floor

close & personal like soft sand
like sap
a saver of light without plenty
—i had nothing to offer

& i offered
it.

A good scripting
given her

Express parsimony
try
any number

No less motion

I had even come down to it

On me knees
asked hidalgo
i was emergency

Older women
made hair

She strafes
at the demonstration

Virginia flag
sweetens me

Spill your upwards cup
for woman of una territory

Makes brakes in the sand
the ocean takes 3 years
to know you

I am the animal i am
there is no vegetating on motion

Something here about thighs
nike
the message loss
look jerky
get big fence
after

I was not with it
that hundreds
to terminal
to terminal a thing
rightly

Mathematics on the lap
of the plane
un avion pulls me
hundreds

old cried woman
on the stair
on the bench
in the plaster
what paperwork?
what more to be done?

Bucked
he did english
tell the people over
overthere
we won't eat no
not not peasant food

Blacker shoes
with
black socks
watches the walking
5 crows
in a row
steeling

I had an
op-
por-
tunity
to opine
i took it
it grew

i tried to
give it back
she swallowed it
running down the stairs
half
naked
half
dressed
this is the truth
this is this fiction
i said
speeding
through numbers
wrens

Cockles
bored her
in the half
shell
tries
by the beaches
switches
of light
oklahoma was bound
to happen

Maestros
up
a green
airplane

tied
outside
where no one can
talk about
her problems

Dizzy hound
settles on
which hand
performs which
acting
my cross
i found her
reading
where the pages
broken
bored
gutted through

An infantile housing
bees make heaven
distant
anchored to ankles
gores the skin
chocolate, lavender, pumice, blond,
sage—this time only

Can you name
the canonical
numbers?

He can.

We are read through
slight slivers
on tiny planes
not enough to make
a grass of

We number
because we can

On the old island
summer to
summer summer
we are ones
falling daily
from the sky
short sumac
compost
oblation

No step
is worth
gingerly
occupies
the plain
i live on
this crowded cloud
where she was coming
from
with those teeth
and that statue

Eat numbly
from the small shell
where the animal

You heard about
drinks
beer
yes
you heard me
numbly eat from
the shell

If you are sitting
if you are not exiting
if you are secure in your
convenance
if you had the time
to tell a crew
from a crowd
from a cloud
from a clod
from clobber
where is your corner
where you are
please,
no light
no more light

The cost
i am too young to
say this
the cost
my love of ocean
my poor
please ignore me

Tuesdays are halt
as cutty timber
where we live
i had risen above once
at a meeting
someone spoke

their song
was full of
cloud
gathered
buffed
formed
boring

Over
io
i owe a lot a money!

She was crying about someone
saying suicide
in public
it wasn't until after
crow's
that i noticed
the green stains
on her green silk pants

Plod
at the party
of ten
your ring alone to go
ach
watching women

drop
from above
realize how formless
when inside them

She gave me
slick children
oh orbit
have you no wheels
i'm walking
i can't
mitigate
in the window
you name the beast,
i'll carry it.

by Dint of kilt
hard-runged belted suppositional

perfume
a Range in newtons

pretty Penumbral no
thickets thick
with shell & clover all over

i am not talking about the sand
are not Wanting to not sit in the window
watching quintain

i wore a slouch
i Hear fine
i misheard the gestural soliloquy

i miss
nothing
i miss
the good news & the Other news

to the
blank to the Rich
stairway

lasso
i had Enough of my world

to pass Around
the party

the Handsome
had some
& then some

bovarian cancer
you don't write This i do
the animal follows the sound

he told me what Happened
what hurt
he had a new name
when he got up

he had Played some
& then some

to Kill a
a empire

a defense of
her English
how i am

same Gain
as my master

squinting russet
the bear would Clock him

elevator gaited
she Approached

we three
intent for rocks—

outside no arno
vecchio & plums—

spent
rose rocks
the way of her garden—

snaps—

at the door
an april
talk to it—

discuss
some holy clown
that city he came from
makes these—

only
i was about the river—

thrown into—

an iceberg on a warming river
outside the museum
in iowa—

she wanted to throw
herself at it
wee content—

duration of clouding
of ou
clotted—

hyacinth hair hyacinth
dressed as where
dressed as
well as
arbited—

are bitten
permit me a clover
changed—

the city people come to change their names in
you are material
suppl'y spoken—

his song of
the ships down—

underwater scavenger
taller woman in another town
waits for it
conditions—

speared & spare
lopez of mine
loping—

great cuties
have you not whispered well
well enough—

jadey
see see—

are you
familiar with muliebrity
pea shooter & the community—

commune
premonitional
road—

had a road it yondered—

how many times seven
are you offered—

preferring not to
your husband(s)
shows no
r—

sends flowers
dalmatians
seasoning—

Quaker meeting today, Alejandra's birthday, red velvet cake, no one spoke today, twice. Twice no one spoke, or is that three now, across the street, shapes of wood, shapes in the wood, that I will catch the dialect, no rage this time like last time at the man the man who stares, Grace caught a firefly in a bag, the mother had no report, Mindy the painter, the women talk afterwards, women talking the woman with the heavy bag, all sound is part of the meeting sound, hammering & buzzing across the street, comes in the room, hits us, is sound, the waiting positions, waiting postures, of sound, more & more no one speaks, heads are arranged downward or up or straight on, I stare at the wood, don't fight says the room to the roomers, borrowed a book. We all wait together in the room, the cat hisses because he hasn't been touched in a long time, my human form that is only the Petitioner. Who is that woman our noisy workshop oblation springs, mankind tigered, 'We are owned men,' ready to walk and not faint. A more subterranean unceasing orientation, we are perpetual, we are perpetually bowed, cleaving meaning to break as well as cling, a universal obligation, they were quickened and called men, Dear Friends, fitful, so to order, that nothing, would crow. About the springs, a mere belief meant to dwell, is the locus, not a problem. We now address ourselves, a sermon on the self-portrait.

nestling the covert attitudes of amazement
marvel the great champion

the woman discovered nebulae
a non-naked planet
who is the focus
of little glances

mingled with a vaster
punctiform
i am given to be in the orbit

we count them as refuse
placed in the shadows
we are happy to pick up a straw

for the love of
of utter poverty
& cling to mammon

war is boring
gee, i punched u

talk about fangs of the mind
these are my paws
that i mentioned

children strangely bleating
it was strong
he was stronger
i'm a radio

can a chest still follow you even
while you're swimming?
woods that end in questions
= deserts
do we have activity

i have harbors
of unfortunate
election

you again

into positions
he maps
opposers

as an accident
an accident

each twist
empirical
from the general

corporal
gathering
cell

biggest toy
space-whatever
struggles
a character

also became strangely
and terribly
luminous

state the rain
endows things
draws it towards
a luminous

the organic
golden
not as

a largest
unity way
a cell

a parallel
cell

don't lean
(appear.)

for wood
invents
the genre

your physical
bone
tries

a solitary
man
a couple

old serbian
old swede
in reverse

mod etcetera
literally familiar
old passive
perhaps
aweather

awnless

hungarian
the consequences
start

and he was fauve

special use
of woman's name

the hospital in
in the public

a place
for the keeping
of a watch
a specialist
a mob
in the canon

they had not been
in this relation
foreign

How many times
have you been
walking
the walk
rose pattern
rising
a cutting
have you been walking.

The earth existed a long time before my birth.

I have never been far from the earth's surface.

Your eyes
are the eyes
close morning
the bee
are dots
the soil
warning.

Still
the rushes
and the incident.

Tincture
of ain't
could a warm view rise
should it.

That woman
on the street
that fetches
fetching bee
that in the air meet
for mating.

13 days to make you.

Their bee
your bee
there bee.

6 bicyclettes
go past me
squares
in an otherwise oval.

When i get to paris
you'll know
paris
when i get there.

In little squares
your hair
in the morning
articulate
snow.

I was thinking
about the elk
·when you called

about the moose
when you called
about the peregrine falcon.

I have only begun
your bestiary.

The orange traipse
this day our mulberry
this day white laundry
in green shadow
like the square
in the circle
in your hand.

Where does the woman go
when she leaves you
where do the women go.

Measuring the women
on the brick
and they will leave you
dusty.

Bruised bee
who has taken
all the salt
from my side.

Plum bruises
you are too right
too near
the original.

In shakes
when your inaudible hair
discretionary
the cobbles
mistook
the street.

Yellow yell
pine bike
in the river.

Stalker of
slower walkers.

He had so long
been george
where the river ended.

When it died
his listened
his children
had better
swallow.

Same tame mary
he lifted
his skirts
and said
some men walk
the street
carrying plates
of sweetthings
for their inner babies.

I
sit a home
count husks
sort shells
fleck bone.

What the driver said
silly with it
the numbers
the crowds
their placement.

Too deep and white
emburied nasty recluse
please prick your neighbor
so that one might
hold fast
to the void.

I beg for you
for the bee

in you
i begged your grave
bigger
white water
waits
these tiny graves.

Look
a panther
his beats
you said
her older sisters
never married
because.

Your eyes
are the eyes
of an army of green
leadrope.

She tied a kilter
on her
arm forces arm
a luxury
of daytime
encoupled.

Moscato, drop glass, sistinic tier, the invention of the visible clock, the invention of street, broken into candle, of the unified sky, down, the corner, there were, dark, in the ark, until stairs.

Because of the intense fabulation, you might as well, betrayed her, oddly body, the button capital, of the world, doesn't it seem like they, should leave a mark on you or something?

It's all about carriage, so I think he'll sing, what are you doing up there?

A mediocre mannerist, they do not want to die, and will not die, they do not die, the nude figure of the foreigner, stress, the last, his priestly quality toward the place of his death represented the episode on the left.

The Nativity was destroyed to make place for the Judgment, handing over of the keys, the fresco is swarming, cut across by a duck in flight, was painted in some of the figures a great square, the importance of windchimes, the leper, the new law.

Dominated & domed, two triumphed faithful copies and the attempted conturbatio, a setsquare, mane of dark hair around his face, and the two animals and the Agony, the Capture refers to the main episode.

An iconographic program could certainly not have been left to the free will of the painters called to carry it out, contains a severe warning.

'I believe he doesn't have the heart for it.'

At the end of bitter were erroneously mentioned, 'it seemed it would not turn out well,' then a 'new commission that I should do what I wanted.'—Michelangelo

An imposing mock, and the Drunkenness, their spandrels typologically to their place, the reason why tree of Jesse a motet, there is no real structural.

'There is no real structural connection between the world of the Seers and that of the Ancestors.'

Objects full of meaning, the Rebel Angels point to their ears, but the witness of the artist has been placed in doubt many times, thinking of my father, looking at the separation of light from darkness, the most articulated, from whom the theologian received his red hat.

A polycentric and moreover a so-called Roman could not have been made from the ground, an extremely irregular surface perforated the ceiling and obtained permission to do what he wanted.

The series of the Seers and the spandrels this was an erection, this structure seen in section, perfectly during the summer months, volcanic dust possessed remarkable knowledge for colours, thanks, members of the team.

A man of whom we know little besides his name, 'one morning he determined to destroy the whole of it' clearly in the putti in the reliefs.

This can be seen in the group of the Children in the Drunkenness in some parts of the Flood and in the Sacrifice, executive timidity, in the use of an outline understood as a limit, around the Drunkenness.

On the islet, the old man figure bearing the body of his son the presence of the assistance, despite local, very accurate, cartoons.

Basically with the one, the one of the Drunkenness, it seems that many were burned following instructions, the dusting powder continued, much was left to inventiveness.

Very quick sketches, generally of small, generally in charcoal or in red chalk but also in pen, in situ, toons, and were of fundamental, the local situation, and making use of nails.

Remained impressed, the master kept only the fugitives on the island, with the exception of some second thoughts, and for the presence of gilding.

Obliged him to work differently, dealing with a ceiling, drafting without body, often very like water, at times thicker and close, at times left, the result is a very luminous, made to be legible in all weathers, and therefore in every light, of an almost maniacal perfection, without harm.

The work proceeded quickly towards the altar.

So too, it is not probably by chance, there is accident, when studies of more than one figure appear on one sheet they always refer to the same.

sierra set
the slow way
we can still die
on a mountain
those people
the ones that
trees forgive
bury it here
in talking mountain.

like diamonds
on a water
in a canyon
corrugated sun sheet
you lie.

we cannot pass
the mountain can
beat sages
their ubiquity
muscle under thrill
he punches
until bloody
that bag.

the passage
the western phone
a sunfelt
wants you
walking.

hit it
we're not over it
yet
two boys
in black shirts
hold hands in the sage
brush
call me when it's over.

been getting
off on platforms
in the sand
junked
heaps of iron helps
three blondes hug
but don't get on
no moving.

the mine was severe
with mists
yellow does it
goes the moon
i never
saw it.

now this
this scape
don't lean
nightness in the mouth
of a cedar
the month the slingtree
don't slash
only sunlight
counts.

rash is
waiting to mount
rock river
behind your caboose
on a plume
that feels
like a string.

pardon the pardoner
the sierric oh no
won't ante up
made *f*'s in the air
made a river
the sordid ouest
lake-smart
tunnel owes
that body water.

notness doesn't mar
rapine tied limb
that i timbered sola
no feat brings me here
no light horn
though the mountain announces.

what kind of blindness?
the work is equal to the work
i am equal to it
and not a daniel.

tell us a horrible horrible horrible story:
after i spoke with you on the
phone everything got better.

fool plum!
i don't want to miss
the story.

very clearly
the sierras are alps
its own despite.

not industrial boy on a cycle
beehive keeps count on the bathetic ground
not technical by numbers
i could train my eye on
all the dead things
all the time.

Sandra Doller (née Miller) is the author of *Oriflamme* (Ahsahta, 2005) and the founder & editrice of *1913* magazine and press. She teaches at Cal State San Marcos and lives way out west with her man, Ben Doller (né Doyle) and their pups Ronald Johnson & Kiki Smith. This is her second book.

Ahsahta Press

Sawtooth Poetry Prize Series

2002: Aaron McCollough, *Welkin* (Brenda Hillman, judge)

2003: Graham Foust, *Leave the Room to Itself* (Joe Wenderoth, judge)

2004: Noah Eli Gordon, *The Area of Sound Called the Subtone* (Claudia Rankine, judge)

2005: Karla Kelsey, *Knowledge, Forms, The Aviary* (Carolyn Forché, judge)

2006: Paige Ackerson-Kiely, *In No One's Land* (D. A. Powell, judge)

2007: Rusty Morrison, *the true keeps calm biding its story* (Peter Gizzi, judge)

2008: Barbara Maloutas, *the whole Marie* (C. D. Wright, judge)

2009: Julie Carr, *100 Notes on Violence* (Rae Armantrout, judge)

New Series

1. Lance Phillips, *Corpus Socius*
2. Heather Sellers, *Drinking Girls and Their Dresses*
3. Lisa Fishman, *Dear, Read*
4. Peggy Hamilton, *Forbidden City*
5. Dan Beachy-Quick, *Spell*
6. Liz Waldner, *Saving the Appearances*
7. Charles O. Hartman, *Island*
8. Lance Phillips, *Cur aliquid vidi*
9. Sandra Miller, *oriflamme.*
10. Brigitte Byrd, *Fence Above the Sea*
11. Ethan Paquin, *The Violence*
12. Ed Allen, *67 Mixed Messages*
13. Brian Henry, *Quarantine*
14. Kate Greenstreet, *case sensitive*
15. Aaron McCollough, *Little Ease*
16. Susan Tichy, *Bone Pagoda*
17. Susan Briante, *Pioneers in the Study of Motion*
18. Lisa Fishman, *The Happiness Experiment*
19. Heidi Lynn Staples, *Dog Girl*
20. David Mutschlecner, *Sign*
21. Kristi Maxwell, *Realm Sixty-four*
22. G. E. Patterson, *To and From*
23. Chris Vitiello, *Irresponsibility*
24. Stephanie Strickland, *Zone : Zero*
25. Charles O. Hartman, *New and Selected Poems*
26. Kathleen Jesme, *The Plum-Stone Game*
27. Ben Doller, *FAQ:*
28. Carrie Olivia Adams, *Intervening Absence*
29. Rachel Loden, *Dick of the Dead*
30. Brigitte Byrd, *Song of a Living Room*
31. Kate Greenstreet, *The Last 4 Things*
32. Brenda Iijima, *If Not Metamorphic*
33. Sandra Doller, *Chora.*
34. Susan Tichy, *Gallowglass*

Ahsahta Press

MODERN AND CONTEMPORARY
POETRY OF THE AMERICAN WEST

This book is set in Apollo MT type
with Helvetica Neue Light titles
by Ahsahta Press at Boise State University
and manufactured according to the Green Press Initiative
by Thomson-Shore, Inc.
Cover design by Quemadura.
Cover art from Yanira Castro's dance and audio installation "(fetus)twin,"
presented at the Chocolate Factory in Long Island City.
Performer: Nancy Ellis. Photograph: Charles Merritt Houghton.
Back cover photograph: Ben Doller
Book design by Janet Holmes.

AHSAHTA PRESS

2010

JANET HOLMES, DIRECTOR

A. MINETTA GOULD

KATE HOLLAND

BREONNA KRAFFT

MERIN TIGERT

JR WALSH

JAKE LUTZ, INTERN

ERIC MARTINEZ, INTERN

NAOMI TARLE, INTERN